Where Is
GOD'S WORD
Today?

A Biblical Proof of the Definitive Authority of the King James Bible

STEPHEN TYNDALE REID

Cover and interior design by Ye Olde Typesetter, Show Low, Arizona, USA 85901
Cover image: Adobe Stock by Oleksandr

Printed in the United States of America

First Edition, Second Printing, 2023

ISBN: 978-1-961110-02-1

Dispensational Publishing House, Inc.
PO Box 3181, Taos, NM 87571
www.dispensationalpublishing.com
Tel: 1 (844) 321-4202

Orders by U.S. trade bookstores and wholesalers. Please contact the publisher:

3 4 5 6 7 8 9 10 1 2

Dedication

This work is dedicated to William Tyndale and the common man for whom he translated the Word of God.

"I defy the Pope and all his laws.
If God spare my life, ere many years
I will cause a boy that driveth the plough
to know more of the Scripture,
than thou dost."
William Tyndale

Table of Contents

1. Introduction

> 2 Timothy 2:15 - Study to shew thyself approved unto God, a workman that needeth not to be ashamed, rightly dividing the word of truth.

Understanding the Bible can be difficult and requires study. If one is not willing to spend time and put forth effort, one will get confused and never come unto the knowledge of the truth (1 Tim. 2:4).

> Proverbs 4:7 - Wisdom *is* the principal thing; *therefore* get wisdom: and with all thy getting get understanding.

> Proverbs 3:13 - Happy is the man *that* findeth wisdom, and the man *that* getteth understanding.

> Proverbs 18:15 - The heart of the prudent getteth knowledge; and the ear of the wise seeketh knowledge.

> Proverbs 19:8 - He that getteth wisdom loveth his own soul: he that keepeth understanding shall find good.

> Proverbs 23:23 - Buy the truth, and sell it not; *also* wisdom, and instruction, and understanding.

When we come to an established understanding of God's Word and obtain wisdom, we will rejoice and have peace.

There is a lot of controversy over the Bible version issue. With plenty of new and supposedly better translations coming out regularly, it can be difficult to determine which version should be used. This study seeks to answer fundamental

questions regarding this issue and defends the King James Version as God's preserved Word for English-speaking people.

> Ecclesiastes 12:12 - And further, by these, my son, be admonished: of making many books *there is* no end; and much study *is* a weariness of the flesh.

There are countless books on Biblical matters. Many will invest their time in these books instead of studying the Bible. While these books can be helpful, they should always be second to reading the Bible itself. After all, why should one read what a scholar thinks over what the Bible itself says? Accordingly, this study is designed to rely on Scripture as its substance and to include little of the author's own thoughts. Nothing herein is meant to be opinion or simply personal insight. Rather, all claims presented are scripturally supported and based on the firm belief that all Scripture is given by inspiration of God, and is profitable for doctrine, for reproof, for correction, for instruction in righteousness: That the man of God may be perfect, throughly furnished unto all good works. (2 Tim. 3:16-17).

Further, this study is intended to be a help to those seeking to locate God's perfect Word so that they may fully trust in the power of God alone and not man's wisdom.

> 1 Corinthians 2:4-5 - And my speech and my preaching *was* not with enticing words of man's wisdom, but in demonstration of the Spirit and of power: 5) That your faith should not stand in the wisdom of men, but in the power of God.

> Acts 17:11 - These were more noble than those in Thessalonica, in that they received the word with all readiness of mind, and searched the scriptures daily, whether those things were so.

Search the Scriptures to see whether these things are so. Do not take someone else's word on such important matters.

2. Prerequisite Beliefs about the Word of God

You may have wondered what version of the Bible you should use. This is a widely debated question, and it may seem like there is no definitive answer. Perhaps you use a version because you like the way it is written, or because your pastor recommended it, or simply because you have grown up with it. It is commonly claimed that no modern English version of the Bible is adequate and that to garner true wisdom you must study Hebrew and Greek. These are all things you have either already heard or likely will hear at some point. This book seeks to address those concerns and answer the fundamental question: what version of the Bible should we use today? Before we address this matter, however, there are a couple of prerequisite truths one must understand about the Word of God in order to think about the issue scripturally.

1. God promised to preserve His Word.

> Psalm 12:6-7 - The words of the LORD *are* pure words: *as* silver tried in a furnace of earth, purified seven times. 7) Thou shalt keep them, O LORD, thou shalt preserve them from this generation for ever.

> Isaiah 40:8 - The grass withereth, the flower fadeth: but the word of our God shall stand for ever.

> Matthew 5:18 - For verily I say unto you, Till heaven and earth pass, one jot or one tittle shall in no wise pass from the law, till all be fulfilled.

> Matthew 24:35 - Heaven and earth shall pass away, but my words shall not pass away.

Mark 13:31 - Heaven and earth shall pass away: but my words shall not pass away.

Luke 16:17 - And it is easier for heaven and earth to pass, than one tittle of the law to fail.

Luke 21:33 - Heaven and earth shall pass away: but my words shall not pass away.

1 Peter 1:25 - But the word of the Lord endureth for ever. And this is the word which by the gospel is preached unto you.

Based on these verses above, there is no doubt that God has promised to preserve His Word. The question then is not *whether* God's Word has been preserved but *where* God's Word has been preserved.

2. The Word of God is necessary for one to have faith.

John 17:17 - Sanctify them through thy truth: thy word is truth.

Romans 10:17 - So then faith *cometh* by hearing, and hearing by the word of God.

For one to be saved, one must hear and believe that Jesus Christ died on the cross for their sins and that salvation is a gift given freely from God (1 Cor. 15:1-4, Eph. 2:8-9). There is nothing we can do to earn it, and once saved, there is no way we can lose it since we are sealed by the Holy Spirit of promise unto the day of redemption (Eph. 1:13, Eph. 4:30).

3. As a soldier of Jesus Christ (2 Tim. 2:3), the Word of God is our weapon. How can we stand for the truth if we do not know where to find our weapon, THE Word of God?

Ephesians 6:17 - And take the helmet of salvation, and the sword of the Spirit, which is the word of God:

2 Corinthians 10:4 - (For the weapons of our warfare *are* not carnal, but mighty through God to the pulling down of strong holds;)

If God's Word is necessary for faith and is also our weapon, it is no surprise that Satan would attempt to corrupt God's Word to weaken the faith and power of those who stand upon its foundation (Eph. 6:10-16, Matt. 7:24-28).

4. We are commanded to study God's Word, and therefore, it matters which Bible we study.

2 Timothy 2:15 - Study to shew thyself approved unto God, a workman that needeth not to be ashamed, rightly dividing the word of truth.

2 Timothy 3:15 - And that from a child thou hast known the holy scriptures, which are able to make thee wise unto salvation through faith which is in Christ Jesus.

As will be demonstrated, there are major differences between versions. Hence, it is crucial we know which Bible God wants us to study.

5. God's name is above all, yet He placed His Word above His name. The importance of God's Word cannot be overstated.

Nehemiah 9:5b - and blessed be thy glorious name, which is exalted above all blessing and praise.

Psalm 138:2b - for thou hast magnified thy word above all thy name.

God is righteous and without flaw, yet His Word has been magnified above even His name. His Word, therefore, must reflect His nature and thus be perfect and without error.

6. God takes false doctrine seriously.

Romans 16:17 - Now I beseech you, brethren, mark them which cause divisions and offences contrary to the doctrine which ye have learned; and avoid them.

Galatians 1:8-9 - But though we, or an angel from heaven, preach any other gospel unto you than that which we have preached unto you, let him be accursed. 9) As we said before, so say I now again, If any *man* preach any other gospel unto you than that ye have received, let him be accursed.

2 Timothy 2:16 - But shun profane *and* vain babblings: for they will increase unto more ungodliness.

Matthew 22:29 - Jesus answered and said unto them, Ye do err, not knowing the scriptures, nor the power of God.

God's perfect justice requires him to punish evil and to correct wrongdoing. In the same way, God does not take false doctrine lightly, as it directly opposes His Word.

The foregoing scriptural truths, if properly applied, will enable us to identify where God's Word is today.

3. Satan's Warfare Against the Word of God

1. No truth can be found in Satan.

> John 8:44 - Ye are of *your* father the devil, and the lusts of your father ye will do. He was a murderer from the beginning, and abode not in the truth, because there is **no truth in him**. When he speaketh a lie, he speaketh of his own: for he is a liar, and the father of it.

2. Satan handles the Word of God deceitfully, misuses it, and changes it.

In the garden, Satan tempted Eve and lied about God's Word. Compare:

> Genesis 2:16-17 - And the LORD God commanded the man, saying, Of every tree of the garden thou **mayest freely eat**: 17) But of the tree of the knowledge of good and evil, **thou shalt not eat of it**: for in the day that thou eatest thereof **thou shalt surely die**.

> Genesis 3:1-4 - Now the serpent was more subtil than any beast of the field which the LORD God had made. And he said unto the woman, Yea, hath God said, Ye shall not eat of every tree of the garden? 2) And the woman said unto the serpent, We **may eat** of the fruit of the trees of the garden: 3) But of the fruit of the tree which *is* in the midst of the garden, God hath said, **Ye shall not eat of it, neither shall ye**

touch it, lest ye die. 4) And the serpent said unto the woman, **Ye shall not surely die**:

Notice the following differences:

God	Woman/Satan
• mayest freely eat	• may eat
• thou shall not eat of it	• Ye shall not eat of it, neither shall ye touch it
• thou shalt surely die	• Ye shall not surely die

The woman adds to and subtracts from the Word of God, and Satan completely opposes it.

3. Satan sets a course to this world and uses doctrines of devils to blind and deceive both unbelievers and believers.

2 Corinthians 4:4 - In whom the god of this world hath blinded the minds of them which believe not, lest the light of the glorious gospel of Christ, who is the image of God, should shine unto them.

Ephesians 2:2 - Wherein in time past ye walked according to the course of this world, according to the prince of the power of the air, the spirit that now worketh in the children of disobedience:

1 Timothy 4:1-2 - Now the Spirit speaketh expressly, that in the latter times some shall depart from the faith, giving heed to seducing spirits, and doctrines of devils; 2) Speaking lies in hypocrisy; having their conscience seared with a hot iron;

Satan is deceptive in his dealings, and since creation, he has always targeted and attempted to corrupt the Word of God. It is no coincidence that there are so many modern versions of the Bible as they result from Satan's efforts to undermine the authority of God's infallible Word.

4. Do All Versions Say the Same Thing?

Although it is often said that modern versions say the same thing as the KJV, this is demonstrably false.

1. **In modern versions, God's nature is degraded, Jesus Christ's deity is diminished, and the Word of God is attacked. Meanwhile, Satan is given exalted titles comparable to Christ. The motive underlying these corruptions is Satan's desire to supplant God and be worshipped.**

   Matthew 4:8-9 - Again, the devil taketh him up into an exceeding high mountain, and sheweth him all the kingdoms of the world, and the glory of them; 9) And saith unto him, All these things will I give thee, if thou wilt fall down and worship me.

   2 Thessalonians 2:4 - Who opposeth and exalteth himself above all that is called God, or that is worshipped; so that he as God sitteth in the temple of God, shewing himself that he is God.

The three-column charts that follow compare the KJV in the left column with the same verse in different modern versions. For brevity's sake, only two modern versions are used to demonstrate the differences, but nearly all examples provided apply to the majority of the newer versions.

Jesus Christ is referred to in Scripture as the "bright and morning star" and the "day star." Notice below how modern versions appropriate language that the KJV uses to refer to the Lord Jesus Christ and apply it to Satan.

> Revelation 22:16 - I Jesus have sent mine angel to testify unto you these things in the churches. I am the root and the offspring of David, *and* the **bright and morning star**.

> 2 Peter 1:19 - We have also a more sure word of prophecy; whereunto ye do well that ye take heed, as unto a light that shineth in a dark place, until the day dawn, and the **day star** arise in your hearts:

Isaiah 14:12 KJV - How art thou fallen from heaven, O **Lucifer**, son of the morning! *how* art thou cut down to the ground, which didst weaken the nations!	Isaiah 14:12 NIV - How you have fallen from heaven, **morning star**, son of the dawn! You have been cast down to the earth, you who once laid low the nations!	Isaiah 14:12 ESV - "How you are fallen from heaven, O **Day Star**, son of Dawn! How you are cut down to the ground, you who laid the nations low!

Just as modern versions exalt Satan, they diminish God by suggesting that it is possible for Him to be deceived.

Psalm 78:36 KJV - Nevertheless **they did flatter him** with their mouth, and they lied unto him with their tongues.	Psalm 78:36 CSB - But **they deceived him** with their mouths, they lied to him with their tongues,	Psalm 78:36 NET - But **they deceived him** with their words, and lied to him.

Modern versions also place a limit on the everlasting nature of God by changing "everlasting" to "ancient times/days" and removing "and art to come."

Micah 5:2 KJV - But thou, Bethlehem Ephratah, *though* thou be little among the thousands of Judah, *yet* out of thee shall he come forth unto me *that is* to be ruler in Israel; whose goings forth *have been* from of old, **from everlasting**.	Micah 5:2 NIV - "But you, Bethlehem Ephrathah, though you are small among the clans of Judah, out of you will come for me one who will be ruler over Israel, whose origins are from of old, **from ancient times**."	Micah 5:2 ESV - But you, O Bethlehem Ephrathah, who are too little to be among the clans of Judah, from you shall come forth for me one who is to be ruler in Israel, whose coming forth is from of old, **from ancient days**.
Revelation 11:17 KJV - Saying, We give thee thanks, O Lord God Almighty, which art, and wast, and **art to come**; because thou hast taken to thee thy great power, and hast reigned.	Revelation 11:17 NIV - saying: "We give thanks to you, Lord God Almighty, the One who is and who was, because you have taken your great power and have begun to reign.	Revelation 11:17 ESV - saying, "We give thanks to you, Lord God Almighty, who is and who was, for you have taken your great power and begun to reign.

Modern versions remove almost an entire verse explaining the trinity.

1 John 5:7 KJV - For there are three that bear record **in heaven, the Father, the Word, and the Holy Ghost: and these three are one**.	1 John 5:7 CSB/ ESV/NASB20/NIV - For there are three that testify:	1 John 5:7 NET - For there are three that testify,

Not only do modern versions denigrate the Father, they also denigrate the Son.

The KJV is correct in saying "her" purification. "Their" purification implies that Jesus had to be purified even though he was sinless and would not be unclean.

Luke 2:22-23 KJV - And when the days of **her purification** according to the law of Moses were accomplished, they brought him to Jerusalem, to present him to the Lord; 23) (As it is written in the law of the Lord, Every male that openeth the womb shall be called holy to the Lord;)	Luke 2:22-23 ESV - And when the time came for **their** purification according to the Law of Moses, they brought him up to Jerusalem to present him to the Lord 23) (as it is written in the Law of the Lord, "Every male who first opens the womb shall be called holy to the Lord")	Luke 2:22-23 ASV - And when the days of **their** purification according to the law of Moses were fulfilled, they brought him up to Jerusalem, to present him to the Lord 23) (as it is written in the law of the Lord, Every male that openeth the womb shall be called holy to the Lord),

God created everything by Jesus Christ. Removing this fact minimizes the role of the Son of God.

Ephesians 3:9 KJV - And to make all *men* see what *is* the fellowship of the mystery, which from the beginning of the world hath been hid in God, who created all things **by Jesus Christ**:	Ephesians 3:9 NIV - and to make plain to everyone the administration of this mystery, which for ages past was kept hidden in God, who created all things.	Ephesians 3:9 CSB - and to shed light for all about the administration of the mystery hidden for ages in God who created all things.

Modern versions' removal of "just" erases Pilate's confirmation to the crowd that Jesus was innocent.

Matthew 27:24 KJV - When Pilate saw that he could prevail nothing, but *that* rather a tumult was made, he took water, and washed *his* hands before the multitude, saying, I am innocent of the blood of this **just** person: see ye *to it.*	Matthew 27:24 NIV - When Pilate saw that he was getting nowhere, but that instead an uproar was starting, he took water and washed his hands in front of the crowd. "I am innocent of this man's blood," he said. "It is your responsibility!"	Matthew 27:24 ESV - So when Pilate saw that he was gaining nothing, but rather that a riot was beginning, he took water and washed his hands before the crowd, saying, "I am innocent of this man's blood; see to it yourselves."

Modern versions omit "yet" and thus make Jesus Christ a liar as he says, "I am not going up to this festival/feast." Meanwhile, verse 10 in all versions states that he goes up to the feast.

John 7:8-10 KJV - Go ye up unto this feast: I go not up **yet** unto this feast; for my time is not yet full come. 9) When he had said these words unto them, he abode *still* in Galilee. 10) But when his brethren were gone up, then went he also up unto the feast, not openly, but as it were in secret.	John 7:8-10 NIV - You go to the festival. I am not going up to this festival, because my time has not yet fully come." 9) After he had said this, he stayed in Galilee. 10) However, after his brothers had left for the festival, he went also, not publicly, but in secret.	John 7:8-10 ESV - You go up to the feast. I am not going up to this feast, for my time has not yet fully come." 9) After saying this, he remained in Galilee. 10) But after his brothers had gone up to the feast, then he also went up, not publicly but in private.

Scripture is clear in all versions that the Lord Jesus Christ demonstrated righteous anger at times.

> Mark 3:5a KJV - And when he had looked round about on them with anger, being grieved for the hardness of their hearts,

> Mark 3:5a NIV - He looked around at them in anger and, deeply distressed at their stubborn hearts,

> Mark 3:5a ESV - He looked around at them in anger and, deeply distressed at their stubborn hearts,

According to modern versions, Jesus Christ is in danger of the judgment.

Matthew 5:22 KJV - But I say unto you, That whosoever is angry with his brother **without a cause** shall be in danger of the judgment: and whosoever shall say to his brother, Raca, shall be in danger of the council: but whosoever shall say, Thou fool, shall be in danger of hell fire.	Matthew 5:22 NIV - But I tell you that anyone who is angry with a brother or sister will be subject to judgment. Again, anyone who says to a brother or sister, 'Raca,' is answerable to the court. And anyone who says, 'You fool!' will be in danger of the fire of hell.	Matthew 5:22 ESV - But I say to you that everyone who is angry with his brother will be liable to judgment; whoever insults his brother will be liable to the council; and whoever says, 'You fool!' will be liable to the hell of fire.

Scripture indicates that the Lord Jesus Christ in His earthly ministry caused righteous division, but modern versions advise its adherents to reject Christ as he was "divisive."

> Luke 12:51 KJV - Suppose ye that I am come to give peace on earth? I tell you, Nay; but rather division:

> Luke 12:51 NKJV - "Do you suppose that I came to give peace on earth? I tell you, not at all, but rather division.

> Luke 12:51 NIV - Do you think I came to bring peace on earth? No, I tell you, but division.

Titus 3:10 KJV - A man that is an **heretick** after the first and second admonition reject;	Titus 3:10 NKJV - Reject a **divisive man** after the first and second admonition,	Titus 3:10 NIV - Warn a **divisive person** once, and then warn them a second time. After that, have nothing to do with them.

The modern versions also attack the power of Christ and His shed blood.

Colossians 1:14 KJV - In whom we have redemption **through his blood**, *even* the forgiveness of sins:	Colossians 1:14 ESV/NIV/RSV - in whom we have redemption, the forgiveness of sins.	Colossians 1:14 CSB - In him we have redemption, the forgiveness of sins.

The word "virgin" does not mean the same thing as "young woman," and such revision, supposedly for the purpose of making the Scriptures easier to understand, actually casts doubt on Christ's immaculate conception.

Isaiah 7:14 KJV - Therefore the Lord himself shall give you a sign; Behold, **a virgin** shall conceive, and bear a son, and shall call his name Immanuel.	Isaiah 7:14 RSV - Therefore the Lord himself will give you a sign. Behold, **a young woman** shall conceive and bear a son, and shall call his name Imman'u-el.	Isaiah 7:14 NET - For this reason the sovereign master himself will give you a confirming sign. Look, **this young woman** is about to conceive and will give birth to a son. You, young woman, will name him Immanuel.

In Luke 2:48-49, Mary attributes the title "father" to Joseph, and Jesus corrects her by calling God His "Father." Modern versions are wrong in describing Joseph as "his father" in contrast to the KJV, which accurately reads "Joseph."

> Luke 2:48-49 - And when they saw him, they were amazed: and his mother said unto him, Son, why hast thou thus dealt with us? behold, thy father and I have sought thee sorrowing. 49) And he said unto them, How is it that ye sought me? wist ye not that I must be about my Father's business?

Luke 2:33 KJV - And **Joseph** and his mother marvelled at those things which were spoken of him.	Luke 2:33 NIV - **The child's father** and mother marveled at what was said about him.	Luke 2:33 ESV - And **his father** and his mother marveled at what was said about him.

Changing "infallible proofs" to "convincing proofs" or simply "proofs" understates the certitude of the proofs the Lord provided.

Acts 1:3 KJV - To whom also he shewed himself alive after his passion by **many infallible proofs**, being seen of them forty days, and speaking of the things pertaining to the kingdom of God:	Acts 1:3 NIV - After his suffering, he presented himself to them and gave **many convincing proofs** that he was alive. He appeared to them over a period of forty days and spoke about the kingdom of God.	Acts 1:3 RSV - To them he presented himself alive after his passion by **many proofs**, appearing to them during forty days, and speaking of the kingdom of God.

Modern verses contain footnotes that express uncertainty as to the authenticity of the first part of Luke 23:34. This casts doubt on perhaps the greatest example of forgiveness ever recorded.

Luke 23:34 KJV - Then said Jesus, Father, forgive them; for they know not what they do. And they parted his raiment, and cast lots.	Luke 23:34 NIV - Jesus said, "Father, forgive them, for they do not know what they are doing." [fn: some early manuscripts do not have this sentence] And they divided up his clothes by casting lots.	Luke 23:34 ESV - And Jesus said, "Father, forgive them, for they know not what they do." [fn: some manuscripts omit the sentence] And they cast lots to divide his garments.

Jesus explains why they will not see him as he will go to the Father. Modern versions remove this information.

John 16:16 KJV - A little while, and ye shall not see me: and again, a little while, and ye shall see me, **because I go to the Father**.	John 16:16 NIV - Jesus went on to say, "In a little while you will see me no more, and then after a little while you will see me."	John 16:16 ESV - "A little while, and you will see me no longer; and again a little while, and you will see me."

They also leave out the Lord's rebuke of Satan.

Luke 4:8 KJV - And Jesus answered and said unto him, **Get thee behind me, Satan**: for it is written, Thou shalt worship the Lord thy God, and him only shalt thou serve.	Luke 4:8 NIV - Jesus answered, "It is written: 'Worship the Lord your God and serve him only.'"	Luke 4:8 ESV - And Jesus answered him, "It is written, "'You shall worship the Lord your God, and him only shall you serve.'"

Below is how each version ends the Gospel of Mark. Most modern versions cast doubt on Mark 16:9-20 by inserting a horizontal line and/or footnote that suggests such verses did not appear in the original autograph, effectively ending the Gospel of Mark with the disciples afraid. The word gospel literally means "good news." Would God write one of His Gospels, which describes the only hope humanity has, and end it with everyone being afraid? The KJV accurately includes Mark 16:9-20, which contains important post-resurrection information.

| Mark 16:20 KJV - And they went forth, and preached every where, the Lord working with *them*, and confirming the word with signs following. Amen. | Mark 16:8 NIV - Trembling and bewildered, the women went out and fled from the tomb. They said nothing to anyone, because they were afraid. | Mark 16:8 ESV - And they went out and fled from the tomb, for trembling and astonishment had seized them, and they said nothing to anyone, for they were afraid. |

The newer versions obscure the Lord's purpose in coming to Earth.

| Luke 9:56 KJV - **For the Son of man is not come to destroy men's lives, but to save them**. And they went to another village. | Luke 9:56 NIV - Then he and his disciples went to another village. | Luke 9:56 ESV - And they went on to another village. |
| Matthew 18:11 KJV - **For the Son of man is come to save that which was lost.** | Matthew 18:11 NIV - [fn: Some manuscripts include here the words of Luke 19:10.] | Matthew 18:11 ESV - [fn: Some manuscripts include here the words of Luke 19:10.] |

When Saul is confronted by the Lord on the road to Damascus, he trembles and is filled with fear. The presence of the Lord is mighty and powerful, and the KJV allows its reader to grasp that. Modern versions remove this, changing and lessening the significance of the appearance of the Lord. They also remove the admonition describing the self-destructive effect of opposing the truth.

Acts 9:5-6 KJV - And he said, Who art thou, Lord? And the Lord said, I am Jesus whom thou persecutest: **it is hard for thee to kick against the pricks. 6) And he trembling and astonished said, Lord, what wilt thou have me to do?** And the Lord *said* unto him, Arise, and go into the city, and it shall be told thee what thou must do.	Acts 9:5-6 NIV - "Who are you, Lord?" Saul asked. "I am Jesus, whom you are persecuting," he replied. 6) "Now get up and go into the city, and you will be told what you must do."	Acts 9:5-6 ESV - And he said, "Who are you, Lord?" And he said, "I am Jesus, whom you are persecuting. 6) But rise and enter the city, and you will be told what you are to do."
Acts 22:9 KJV - And they that were with me saw indeed the light, **and were afraid**; but they heard not the voice of him that spake to me.	Acts 22:9 NIV - My companions saw the light, but they did not understand the voice of him who was speaking to me.	Acts 22:9 ESV - Now those who were with me saw the light but did not understand the voice of the one who was speaking to me.

Modern versions cut out many key details of the Lord's prayer as recorded in Matthew 6 and Luke 11.

Matthew 6:13 KJV - And lead us not into temptation, but deliver us from evil: **For thine is the kingdom, and the power, and the glory, for ever. Amen**.	Matthew 6:13 NIV - And lead us not into temptation, but deliver us from the evil one.'	Matthew 6:13 ESV - And lead us not into temptation, but deliver us from evil.
Luke 11:2-4 KJV - And he said unto them, When ye pray, say, Our Father which art **in heaven**, Hallowed be thy name. Thy kingdom come. **Thy will be done, as in heaven, so in earth**. 3) Give us day by day our daily bread. 4) And forgive us our sins; for we also forgive every one that is indebted to us. And lead us not into temptation; **but deliver us from evil**.	Luke 11:2-4 NIV - He said to them, "When you pray, say: " 'Father, hallowed be your name, your kingdom come. 3) Give us each day our daily bread. 4) Forgive us our sins, for we also forgive everyone who sins against us. And lead us not into temptation.' "	Luke 11:2-4 ESV - And he said to them, "When you pray, say: "Father, hallowed be your name. Your kingdom come. 3) Give us each day our daily bread, 4) and forgive us our sins, for we ourselves forgive everyone who is indebted to us. And lead us not into temptation."

Modern versions remove the description of the Lord as everlasting in Revelation 5:14.

Revelation 5:14 KJV - And the four beasts said, Amen. And the four *and* twenty elders fell down and worshipped **him that liveth for ever and ever**.	Revelation 5:14 NIV - The four living creatures said, "Amen," and the elders fell down and worshiped.	Revelation 5:14 ESV - And the four living creatures said, "Amen!" and the elders fell down and worshiped.

The modern versions transform the unique earthly ministry of the Lord Jesus Christ into a collective effort that includes the disciples.

John 9:4 KJV - **I** must work the works of him that sent me, while it is day: the night cometh, when no man can work.	John 9:4 NIV - As long as it is day, **we** must do the works of him who sent me. Night is coming, when no one can work.	John 9:4 ESV - **We** must work the works of him who sent me while it is day; night is coming, when no one can work.

The following examples show how modern versions attack the word of God.

Saying "Every scripture inspired of/by God" implies there is some Scripture that is not inspired by God and undermines the authority of God's Word.

2 Timothy 3:16 KJV - **All scripture is given by inspiration of God**, and is profitable for doctrine, for reproof, for correction, for instruction in righteousness:	2 Timothy 3:16 ASV - **Every scripture inspired of God** is also profitable for teaching, for reproof, for correction, for instruction which is in righteousness:	2 Timothy 3:16 HNV - **Every writing inspired by God** is profitable for teaching, for reproof, for correction, and for instruction which is in righteousness,

Modern translations undermine the doctrine of inspiration.

Jeremiah 23:30 KJV - Therefore, behold, I am against the prophets, saith the LORD, that steal **my words** every one from his neighbour.	Jeremiah 23:30 NIV - "Therefore," declares the LORD, "I am against the prophets who steal from one another words **supposedly from me**.	Jeremiah 23:30 NET - So I, the LORD, affirm that I am opposed to those prophets who steal messages from one another that **they claim are from me**.

Ironically, the modern versions remove the reference to "every word of God" in a key verse that emphasizes the importance of every word. In doing this, they leave out the main point that Luke 4:4 should be making in quoting Deuteronomy 8:3. It is hard to imagine a clearer proof that modern versions undermine the authority of the Scriptures.

Deuteronomy 8:3 KJV - And he humbled thee, and suffered thee to hunger, and fed thee with manna, which thou knewest not, neither did thy fathers know; that he might make thee know that man doth not live by bread only, **but by every *word* that proceedeth out of the mouth of the LORD doth man live**.	Deuteronomy 8:3 NIV - He humbled you, causing you to hunger and then feeding you with manna, which neither you nor your ancestors had known, to teach you that man does not live on bread alone **but on every word that comes from the mouth of the LORD**.	Deuteronomy 8:3 ESV - And he humbled you and let you hunger and fed you with manna, which you did not know, nor did your fathers know, that he might make you know that man does not live by bread alone, **but man lives by every word that comes from the mouth of the LORD**.
Luke 4:4 KJV - And Jesus answered him, saying, It is written, That man shall not live by bread alone, **but by every word of God**.	Luke 4:4 NIV - Jesus answered, "It is written: 'Man shall not live on bread alone.'"	Luke 4:4 ESV - And Jesus answered him, "It is written, 'Man shall not live by bread alone.'"

2. There are many substantive differences between the King James Bible and modern versions, all of which prove the accuracy of the KJV.

The King James Version is correct in saying that Elhanan killed the brother of Goliath and not Goliath as everyone knows that David killed Goliath. Modern versions contradict themselves in 1 Chronicles 20, which describes the same events as 2 Samuel 21.

2 Samuel 21:19 KJV - And there was again a battle in Gob with the Philistines, where **Elhanan** the son of Jaareoregim, a Bethlehemite, **slew *the brother of Goliath the Gittite***, the staff of whose spear *was* like a weaver's beam.	2 Samuel 21:19 ESV - And there was again war with the Philistines at Gob, and **Elhanan** the son of Jaare-oregim, the Bethlehemite, **struck down Goliath the Gittite**, the shaft of whose spear was like a weaver's beam.	2 Samuel 21:19 CSB - Once again there was a battle with the Philistines at Gob, and **Elhanan** son of Jaare-oregim the Bethlehemite **killed Goliath of Gath**. The shaft of his spear was like a weaver's beam.
1 Chronicles 20:5 KJV - And there was war again with the Philistines; and **Elhanan** the son of Jair **slew Lahmi the brother of Goliath the Gittite**, whose spear staff *was* like a weaver's beam.	1 Chronicles 20:5 ESV - And there was again war with the Philistines, and **Elhanan** the son of Jair **struck down Lahmi the brother of Goliath the Gittite**, the shaft of whose spear was like a weaver's beam.	1 Chronicles 20:5 CSB - Once again there was a battle with the Philistines, and **Elhanan** son of Jair **killed Lahmi the brother of Goliath of Gath**. The shaft of his spear was like a weaver's beam.

In Numbers 32, both the KJV and modern versions accurately state that all of Israel rebelled except Caleb and Joshua. However, in Hebrews 3, the modern versions denounce the faith of Caleb and Joshua by saying that all of Israel rebelled and therefore contradict themselves. In contrast, the KJV correctly states that it was "not all" that rebelled in the wilderness.

| Numbers 32:11-12 KJV - Surely none of the men that came up out of Egypt, from twenty years old and upward, shall see the land which I sware unto Abraham, unto Isaac, and unto Jacob; because they have not wholly followed me: 12) Save Caleb the son of Jephunneh the Kenezite, and Joshua the son of Nun: for they have wholly followed the LORD. | Numbers 32:11-12 NIV - 'Because they have not followed me wholeheartedly, not one of those who were twenty years old or more when they came up out of Egypt will see the land I promised on oath to Abraham, Isaac and Jacob— 12) not one except Caleb son of Jephunneh the Kenizzite and Joshua son of Nun, for they followed the LORD wholeheartedly.' | Numbers 32:11-12 RSV - 'Surely none of the men who came up out of Egypt, from twenty years old and upward, shall see the land which I swore to give to Abraham, to Isaac, and to Jacob, because they have not wholly followed me; 12) none except Caleb the son of Jephun'neh the Ken'izzite and Joshua the son of Nun, for they have wholly followed the LORD.' |

Hebrews 3:15-16 KJV - While it is said, To day if ye will hear his voice, harden not your hearts, as in the provocation. 16) For some, when they had heard, did provoke: **howbeit not all** that came out of Egypt by Moses.	Hebrews 3:15-16 NIV - As has just been said: "Today, if you hear his voice, do not harden your hearts as you did in the rebellion." 16) Who were they who heard and rebelled? **Were they not all** those Moses led out of Egypt?	Hebrews 3:15-16 RSV - while it is said, "Today, when you hear his voice, do not harden your hearts as in the rebellion." 16) Who were they that heard and yet were rebellious? **Was it not all** those who left Egypt under the leadership of Moses?

In Deuteronomy 7, the Lord clearly instructed Israel to burn the graven images of the false gods with fire. The account of 2 Samuel 5 shows us that David and his men obeyed God and burnt them. Modern versions change "burned them" to "carried them off/away." This casts doubt on the faithfulness of David. Did he burn them, or did he take them with him as Rachel took Laban's gods in Genesis 31? Modern versions consistently confuse the meaning of clear, simple passages.

> Deuteronomy 7:5 - But thus shall ye deal with them; ye shall destroy their altars, and break down their images, and cut down their groves, and burn their graven images with fire.

> Deuteronomy 7:25 - The graven images of their gods shall ye burn with fire: thou shalt not desire the silver or gold *that is* on them, nor take *it* unto thee, lest thou be snared therein: for it *is* an abomination to the LORD thy God.

| 2 Samuel 5:20-21 KJV - And David came to Baalperazim, and David smote them there, and said, The LORD hath broken forth upon mine enemies before me, as the breach of waters. Therefore he called the name of that place Baalperazim. 21) **And there they left their images, and David and his men burned them**. | 2 Samuel 5:20-21 NIV - So David went to Baal Perazim, and there he defeated them. He said, "As waters break out, the LORD has broken out against my enemies before me." So that place was called Baal Perazim. 21) **The Philistines abandoned their idols there, and David and his men carried them off**. | 2 Samuel 5:20-21 ESV - And David came to Baal-perazim, and David defeated them there. And he said, "The LORD has broken through my enemies before me like a breaking flood." Therefore the name of that place is called Baal-perazim. 21) **And the Philistines left their idols there, and David and his men carried them away**. |

Mark 1:2 quotes Malachi 3:1, and Mark 1:3 quotes Isaiah 40:3. Thus, two different prophets are quoted. Accordingly, the KJV accurately refers to "the prophets," while modern versions inaccurately attribute both quotes to "Isaiah the prophet." The KJV is correct in saying "the prophets."

> Malachi 3:1 - Behold, I will send my messenger, and he shall prepare the way before me: and the Lord, whom ye seek, shall suddenly come to his temple, even the messenger of the covenant, whom ye delight in: behold, he shall come, saith the LORD of hosts.

> Isaiah 40:3 - The voice of him that crieth in the wilderness, Prepare ye the way of the LORD, make straight in the desert a highway for our God.

Mark 1:2-3 KJV - As it is written in **the prophets**, Behold, I send my messenger before thy face, which shall prepare thy way before thee. 3) The voice of one crying in the wilderness, Prepare ye the way of the Lord, make his paths straight.	Mark 1:2-3 NIV - as it is written in **Isaiah the prophet**: "I will send my messenger ahead of you, who will prepare your way"– 3) "a voice of one calling in the wilderness, 'Prepare the way for the Lord, make straight paths for him.' "	Mark 1:2-3 ESV - As it is written in **Isaiah the prophet**, "Behold, I send my messenger before your face, who will prepare your way, 3) the voice of one crying in the wilderness: 'Prepare the way of the Lord, make his paths straight,'"

One is either saved or not saved. There is no such thing as "are being saved." The modern versions teach a false gospel.

1 Corinthians 1:18 KJV - For the preaching of the cross is to them that perish foolishness; but unto us which **are saved** it is the power of God.	1 Corinthians 1:18 NKJV - For the message of the cross is foolishness to those who are perishing, but to us who **are being saved** it is the power of God.	1 Corinthians 1:18 NIV - For the message of the cross is foolishness to those who are perishing, but to us who **are being saved** it is the power of God.
Hebrews 10:14 KJV - For by one offering he hath perfected for ever them that **are sanctified**.	Hebrews 10:14 NKJV - For by one offering He has perfected forever those who **are being sanctified**.	Hebrews 10:14 ESV - For by a single offering he has perfected for all time those who **are being sanctified**.

It is not enough to believe whatever one wants; one must believe on the Lord Jesus Christ.

John 6:47 KJV - Verily, verily, I say unto you, He that believeth **on me** hath everlasting life.	John 6:47 NIV - Very truly I tell you, the one who believes has eternal life.	John 6:47 ESV - Truly, truly, I say to you, whoever believes has eternal life.

When we deny Christ, we do not lose our salvation; rather, we may lose reward and the opportunity to reign with Him.

2 Timothy 2:12 KJV - If we suffer, we shall also reign with *him*: if we deny *him*, he also will **deny us:**	2 Timothy 2:12 NIV - if we endure, we will also reign with him. If we disown him, he will also **disown us;**	2 Timothy 2:12 GW - If we endure, we will rule with him. If we disown him, he will **disown us.**

Modern versions falsely state that the wicked person's ways are always "prospering/secure."

Psalm 10:4-5 KJV - The wicked, through the pride of his countenance, will not seek *after God*: God *is* not in all his thoughts. 5) **His ways are always grievous;** thy judgments *are* far above out of his sight: *as for* all his enemies, he puffeth at them.	Psalm 10:4-5 NKJV - The wicked in his proud countenance does not seek *God*; God *is* in none of his thoughts. 5) **His ways are always prospering;** Your judgments *are* far above, out of his sight; *As for* all his enemies, he sneers at them.	Psalm 10:4-5 CSB - In all his scheming, the wicked person arrogantly thinks, "There's no accountability, since there's no God." 5) **His ways are always secure;** your lofty judgments have no effect on him; he scoffs at all his adversaries.

Reflecting the covetousness of our time, modern versions omit the Lord's warning about trusting in riches.

Mark 10:24 KJV - And the disciples were astonished at his words. But Jesus answereth again, and saith unto them, Children, how hard is it for them **that trust in riches** to enter into the kingdom of God!	Mark 10:24 NIV - The disciples were amazed at his words. But Jesus said again, "Children, how hard it is to enter the kingdom of God!	Mark 10:24 ESV - And the disciples were amazed at his words. But Jesus said to them again, "Children, how difficult it is to enter the kingdom of God!

They do not know the day nor the hour of what? The KJV is specific and understandable.

Matthew 25:13 KJV - Watch therefore, for ye know neither the day nor the hour **wherein the Son of man cometh**.	Matthew 25:13 NIV - "Therefore keep watch, because you do not know the day or the hour.	Matthew 25:13 ESV - Watch therefore, for you know neither the day nor the hour.

Modern versions obscure and confuse the fourth person in the fiery furnace.

Daniel 3:25 KJV - He answered and said, Lo, I see four men loose, walking in the midst of the fire, and they have no hurt; and the form of the fourth is like **the Son of God**.	Daniel 3:25 NIV - He said, "Look! I see four men walking around in the fire, unbound and unharmed, and the fourth looks like **a son of the gods**."	Daniel 3:25 ESV - He answered and said, "But I see four men unbound, walking in the midst of the fire, and they are not hurt; and the appearance of the fourth is like **a son of the gods**."

The KJV explains why the angel commanded Cornelius to send men to Joppa. Meanwhile, modern versions leave the reader uninformed.

Acts 10:4-6 KJV	Acts 10:4-6 NIV	Acts 10:4-6 ESV
- And when he looked on him, he was afraid, and said, What is it, Lord? And he said unto him, Thy prayers and thine alms are come up for a memorial before God. 5) And now send men to Joppa, and call for *one* Simon, whose surname is Peter: 6) He lodgeth with one Simon a tanner, whose house is by the sea side: **he shall tell thee what thou oughtest to do**.	- Cornelius stared at him in fear. "What is it, Lord?" he asked. The angel answered, "Your prayers and gifts to the poor have come up as a memorial offering before God. 5) Now send men to Joppa to bring back a man named Simon who is called Peter. 6) He is staying with Simon the tanner, whose house is by the sea."	- And he stared at him in terror and said, "What is it, Lord?" And he said to him, "Your prayers and your alms have ascended as a memorial before God. 5) And now send men to Joppa and bring one Simon who is called Peter. 6) He is lodging with one Simon, a tanner, whose house is by the sea."

Acts 10:31-32 KJV - And said, Cornelius, thy prayer is heard, and thine alms are had in remembrance in the sight of God. 32) Send therefore to Joppa, and call hither Simon, whose surname is Peter; he is lodged in the house of *one* Simon a tanner by the sea side: **who, when he cometh, shall speak unto thee**.	Acts 10:31-32 NIV - and said, 'Cornelius, God has heard your prayer and remembered your gifts to the poor. 32) Send to Joppa for Simon who is called Peter. He is a guest in the home of Simon the tanner, who lives by the sea.'	Acts 10:31-32 ESV - and said, 'Cornelius, your prayer has been heard and your alms have been remembered before God. 32) Send therefore to Joppa and ask for Simon who is called Peter. He is lodging in the house of Simon, a tanner, by the sea.'

Modern versions remove both the gospel presentation to and the testimony of the Ethiopian eunuch.

Acts 8:37 KJV - And Philip said, **If thou believest with all thine heart, thou mayest. And he answered and said, I believe that Jesus Christ is the Son of God**.	Acts 8:37 NIV - [fn]	Acts 8:37 ESV - [fn]

On his own, man cannot purify his soul. He needs the Spirit's help.

1 Peter 1:22 KJV - Seeing ye have purified your souls in obeying the truth **through the Spirit** unto unfeigned love of the brethren, *see that ye* love one another with a pure heart fervently:	1 Peter 1:22 NIV - Now that you have purified yourselves by obeying the truth so that you have sincere love for each other, love one another deeply, from the heart.	1 Peter 1:22 ESV - Having purified your souls by your obedience to the truth for a sincere brotherly love, love one another earnestly from a pure heart,

After learning the salvation of God was being sent to the Gentiles, the Jews had great reasoning among themselves as to what this meant for them since they were God's chosen people. This significant event is omitted from modern versions.

Acts 28:28-29 KJV - Be it known therefore unto you, that the salvation of God is sent unto the Gentiles, and *that* they will hear it. 29) **And when he had said these words, the Jews departed, and had great reasoning among themselves.**	Acts 28:28-29 NIV - "Therefore I want you to know that God's salvation has been sent to the Gentiles, and they will listen!" 29) [fn]	Acts 28:28-29 ESV - Therefore let it be known to you that this salvation of God has been sent to the Gentiles; they will listen." 29) [fn]

The KJV contains two parallel statements that demonstrate the mutually exclusive nature of grace and works for justification, but newer versions remove the latter half of the comparison.

Romans 11:6 KJV - And if by grace, then *is it* no more of works: otherwise grace is no more grace. **But if** *it be* **of works, then is it no more grace: otherwise work is no more work**.	Romans 11:6 NIV - And if by grace, then it cannot be based on works; if it were, grace would no longer be grace.	Romans 11:6 ESV - But if it is by grace, it is no longer on the basis of works; otherwise grace would no longer be grace.

Removing the latter half of the first sentence of Romans 14:6 is an example of how newer versions omit information that is necessary for complete understanding.

Romans 14:6 KJV - He that regardeth the day, regardeth *it* unto the Lord; **and he that regardeth not the day, to the Lord he doth not regard it**. He that eateth, eateth to the Lord, for he giveth God thanks; and he that eateth not, to the Lord he eateth not, and giveth God thanks.	Romans 14:6 NIV - Whoever regards one day as special does so to the Lord. Whoever eats meat does so to the Lord, for they give thanks to God; and whoever abstains does so to the Lord and gives thanks to God.	Romans 14:6 ESV - The one who observes the day, observes it in honor of the Lord. The one who eats, eats in honor of the Lord, since he gives thanks to God, while the one who abstains, abstains in honor of the Lord and gives thanks to God.

The exclusion at the end of 1 Corinthians 6:20 deletes an important teaching that the believer should glorify God in both body and spirit.

1 Corinthians 6:20 KJV - For ye are bought with a price: therefore glorify God in your body, **and in your spirit, which are God's**.	1 Corinthians 6:20 NIV - you were bought at a price. Therefore honor God with your bodies.	1 Corinthians 6:20 ESV - for you were bought with a price. So glorify God in your body.

Modern versions leave out the direct command in 1 Timothy 6:5 to withdraw from those of corrupt minds.

1 Timothy 6:5 KJV - Perverse disputings of men of corrupt minds, and destitute of the truth, supposing that gain is godliness: **from such withdraw thyself**.	1 Timothy 6:5 NIV - and constant friction between people of corrupt mind, who have been robbed of the truth and who think that godliness is a means to financial gain.	1 Timothy 6:5 NLT - These people always cause trouble. Their minds are corrupt, and they have turned their backs on the truth. To them, a show of godliness is just a way to become wealthy.

The KJV provides greater detail than modern versions on how to love our enemies.

Matthew 5:44 KJV - But I say unto you, Love your enemies, **bless them that curse you, do good to them that hate you**, and pray for them which **despitefully use you**, and persecute you;	Matthew 5:44 NIV - But I tell you, love your enemies and pray for those who persecute you,	Matthew 5:44 ESV - But I say to you, Love your enemies and pray for those who persecute you,

Scripture instructs us not simply to refrain from evil but also the appearance of evil. The modern versions omit this truth.

1 Thessalonians 5:22 KJV - Abstain from all **appearance** of evil.	1 Thessalonians 5:22 NKJV - Abstain from every form of evil.	1 Thessalonians 5:22 NIV - reject every kind of evil.

Modern versions take out the command to study and confuse a clarifying point on how to study: "rightly dividing the word of truth."

2 Timothy 2:15 KJV - **Study** to shew thyself approved unto God, a workman that needeth not to be ashamed, **rightly dividing the word of truth**.	2 Timothy 2:15 NIV - **Do your best** to present yourself to God as one approved, a worker who does not need to be ashamed and who **correctly handles the word of truth**.	2 Timothy 2:15 ESV - **Do your best** to present yourself to God as one approved, a worker who has no need to be ashamed, **rightly handling the word of truth**.

The modern versions promote talebearing when they describe the words of a talebearer as "tasty trifles" and "delicious morsels," instead of what they really are – "wounds."

Proverbs 26:22 KJV - The words of a talebearer *are* as **wounds**, and they go down into the innermost parts of the belly.	Proverbs 26:22 NKJV - The words of a talebearer *are* like **tasty trifles**, And they go down into the inmost body.	Proverbs 26:22 ESV - The words of a whisperer are like **delicious morsels**; they go down into the inner parts of the body.

In John 8:9, the scribes and Pharisees did not leave simply because they "heard." They left due to the conviction of their conscience.

John 8:9 KJV - And they which heard it, **being convicted by *their own* conscience**, went out one by one, beginning at the eldest, even unto the last: and Jesus was left alone, and the woman standing in the midst.	John 8:9 NIV - At this, those who heard began to go away one at a time, the older ones first, until only Jesus was left, with the woman still standing there.	John 8:9 ESV - But when they heard it, they went away one by one, beginning with the older ones, and Jesus was left alone with the woman standing before him.

In Colossians 2:18, the modern versions falsely read "have/ hath seen" which is the exact opposite of "hath not seen."

Colossians 2:18 KJV - Let no man beguile you of your reward in a voluntary humility and worshipping of angels, **intruding into those things which he hath not seen**, vainly puffed up by his fleshly mind,	Colossians 2:18 NIV - Do not let anyone who delights in false humility and the worship of angels disqualify you. Such a person also **goes into great detail about what they have seen**; they are puffed up with idle notions by their unspiritual mind.	Colossians 2:18 ASV - Let no man rob you of your prize by a voluntary humility and worshipping of the angels, **dwelling in the things which he hath seen**, vainly puffed up by his fleshly mind,

In Matthew 25:31, modern versions omit the word "holy" and therefore fail to distinguish between the holy angels and those that fell.

Matthew 25:31 KJV - When the Son of man shall come in his glory, and all the **holy** angels with him, then shall he sit upon the throne of his glory:	Matthew 25:31 NIV - "When the Son of Man comes in his glory, and all the angels with him, he will sit on his glorious throne.	Matthew 25:31 ESV - "When the Son of Man comes in his glory, and all the angels with him, then he will sit on his glorious throne.

A simple word search will confirm that "Calvary" is completely removed from nearly all modern versions and replaced with "the Skull."

Luke 23:33 KJV - And when they were come to the place, which is called **Calvary**, there they crucified him, and the malefactors, one on the right hand, and the other on the left.	Luke 23:33 NIV - When they came to the place called **the Skull**, they crucified him there, along with the criminals—one on his right, the other on his left.	Luke 23:33 ESV - And when they came to the place that is called **The Skull**, there they crucified him, and the criminals, one on his right and one on his left.

Modern versions place John 5:4 in a footnote and thus relegate the explanation necessary to understand the passage.

John 5:3-4 KJV	John 5:3-4 NIV	John 5:3-4 ESV
- In these lay a great multitude of impotent folk, of blind, halt, withered, waiting for the moving of the water. 4) **For an angel went down at a certain season into the pool, and troubled the water: whosoever then first after the troubling of the water stepped in was made whole of whatsoever disease he had**.	- Here a great number of disabled people used to lie—the blind, the lame, the paralyzed. 4) [fn]	- In these lay a multitude of invalids—blind, lame, and paralyzed. 4) [fn]

Modern versions remove Mark 9:44 and 46 completely, as well as the end of verse 45. Is God not allowed to repeat himself to stress a point? It is clear in the KJV that hell is horrific and that the fire shall never be quenched. Scripture purposely repeats itself to make sure the reader understands the gravity of the situation. Modern versions weaken the Lord's warnings.

Mark 9:44-48 KJV	Mark 9:44-48 NIV	Mark 9:44-48 ESV
- **Where their worm dieth not, and the fire is not quenched**. 45) And if thy foot offend thee, cut it off: it is better for thee to enter halt into life, than having two feet to be cast into hell, **into the fire that never shall be quenched**: 46) **Where their worm dieth not, and the fire is not quenched**. 47) And if thine eye offend thee, pluck it out: it is better for thee to enter into the kingdom of God with one eye, than having two eyes to be cast into hell **fire**: 48) **Where their worm dieth not, and the fire is not quenched**.	- [fn] 45) And if your foot causes you to stumble, cut it off. It is better for you to enter life crippled than to have two feet and be thrown into hell. 46) [fn] 47) And if your eye causes you to stumble, pluck it out. It is better for you to enter the kingdom of God with one eye than to have two eyes and be thrown into hell, 48) **where " 'the worms that eat them do not die, and the fire is not quenched.'**	- [fn] 45) And if your foot causes you to sin, cut it off. It is better for you to enter life lame than with two feet to be thrown into hell. 46) [fn] 47) And if your eye causes you to sin, tear it out. It is better for you to enter the kingdom of God with one eye than with two eyes to be thrown into hell, 48) **'where their worm does not die and the fire is not quenched.'**

Removing "should not perish" from John 3:15 is another instance of modern versions discarding the Lord's caution to unbelievers.

John 3:15 KJV - That whosoever believeth in him **should not perish**, but have eternal life.	John 3:15 NIV - that everyone who believes may have eternal life in him."	John 3:15 ESV - that whoever believes in him may have eternal life.

Despite how modern versions read in Revelation 21:24, not all of the nations are saved.

Revelation 21:24 KJV - And the nations of them **which are saved** shall walk in the light of it: and the kings of the earth do bring their glory and honour into it.	Revelation 21:24 NIV - The nations will walk by its light, and the kings of the earth will bring their splendor into it.	Revelation 21:24 ESV - By its light will the nations walk, and the kings of the earth will bring their glory into it,

Modern versions obscure God's presence and the fact that the lost will stand in judgment before God.

Revelation 14:5 KJV - And in their mouth was found no guile: for they are without fault **before the throne of God**.	Revelation 14:5 NIV - No lie was found in their mouths; they are blameless.	Revelation 14:5 ESV - and in their mouth no lie was found, for they are blameless.
Revelation 20:9 KJV - And they went up on the breadth of the earth, and compassed the camp of the saints about, and the beloved city: and fire came down **from God** out of heaven, and devoured them.	Revelation 20:9 NIV - They marched across the breadth of the earth and surrounded the camp of God's people, the city he loves. But fire came down from heaven and devoured them.	Revelation 20:9 ESV - And they marched up over the broad plain of the earth and surrounded the camp of the saints and the beloved city, but fire came down from heaven and consumed them,
Revelation 20:12 KJV - And I saw the dead, small and great, stand **before God**; and the books were opened: and another book was opened, which is the book of life: and the dead were judged out of those things which were written in the books, according to their works.	Revelation 20:12 NIV - And I saw the dead, great and small, standing before the throne, and books were opened. Another book was opened, which is the book of life. The dead were judged according to what they had done as recorded in the books.	Revelation 20:12 ESV - And I saw the dead, great and small, standing before the throne, and books were opened. Then another book was opened, which is the book of life. And the dead were judged by what was written in the books, according to what they had done.

Modern translators omit one of the ten commandments quoted in Romans 13:9. Ironically, it is the commandment against bearing false witness.

Romans 13:9 KJV - For this, Thou shalt not commit adultery, Thou shalt not kill, Thou shalt not steal, **Thou shalt not bear false witness**, Thou shalt not covet; and if *there be* any other commandment, it is briefly comprehended in this saying, namely, Thou shalt love thy neighbour as thyself.	Romans 13:9 NIV - The commandments, "You shall not commit adultery," "You shall not murder," "You shall not steal," "You shall not covet," and whatever other command there may be, are summed up in this one command: "Love your neighbor as yourself."	Romans 13:9 ESV - For the commandments, "You shall not commit adultery, You shall not murder, You shall not steal, You shall not covet," and any other commandment, are summed up in this word: "You shall love your neighbor as yourself."

Modern versions revise "corrupt" to "peddle" in 2 Corinthians 2:17 and thus engage in the very behavior the verse condemns.

2 Corinthians 2:17 KJV - For we are not as many, which **corrupt the word of God**: but as of sincerity, but as of God, in the sight of God speak we in Christ.	2 Corinthians 2:17 NKJV - For we are not, as so many, **peddling the word of God**; but as of sincerity, but as from God, we speak in the sight of God in Christ.	2 Corinthians 2:17 NIV - Unlike so many, we do not **peddle the word of God** for profit. On the contrary, in Christ we speak before God with sincerity, as those sent from God.

3. Missing Words

Scripture is clear that one should not add to or subtract from God's Word.

> Deuteronomy 4:2 - Ye shall not add unto the word which I command you, neither shall ye diminish *ought* from it, that ye may keep the commandments of the LORD your God which I command you.

> Deuteronomy 12:32 - What thing soever I command you, observe to do it: thou shalt not add thereto, nor diminish from it.

> Proverbs 30:5-6 - Every word of God *is* pure: he *is* a shield unto them that put their trust in him. 6) Add thou not unto his words, lest he reprove thee, and thou be found a liar.

> Revelation 22:19 - And if any man shall take away from the words of the book of this prophecy, God shall take away his part out of the book of life, and out of the holy city, and *from* the things which are written in this book.

Although the exact figures vary, the versions below are commonly estimated to have the following approximate word counts:

KJV – ~783,000 words[1]	NIV – ~728,000 words[2]	ESV – ~757,000 words[3]

Thus, the NIV removes ~55,000 words and the ESV removes ~26,000 words as compared to the KJV.

---

1   Allison Dexter, "How Many Words Are in the Bible? - Word Counter," - Word Counter (Wasai, July 11, 2022), https://wordcounter.io/blog/how-many-words-are-in-the-bible.
2   Id.
3   "Concordance," ESV Bible, accessed February 27, 2023, https://www.esv.org/resources/esv-global-study-bible/concordance/.

All of this demonstrates a pattern. Modern versions degrade God's nature, diminish the deity of Christ, apply exalted titles to Satan, confuse clear passages, omit necessary information, corrupt the gospel, and introduce blatant contradictions into the text. Our earlier analysis of God's numerous promises of preservation showed that the question is not *whether* God has preserved His Word, but *where* God has preserved His Word. With regard to the English language, it is more than obvious that God has preserved His Word in the King James Version.

Modern versions of the Bible have very stark changes in meaning compared to the KJV. As the numerous examples above have shown, it is obvious that the KJV is the accurate, precise, and trustworthy version.

5. Do the Differences in Versions Matter?

The short answer is yes.

There is a common misconception that Bible versions say the same thing and do not vary in doctrinal content. While this view is widely held, it is incorrect.

We have already seen that the differences are not subtle nuances, but complete changes in meaning. Saying the differences are minute or insignificant is a misunderstanding of the issue. Satan knows that there is only so much he can corrupt in a version before it is not accepted. For instance, if a Bible version directly stated, "Jesus is a sinner," such version would be rejected by nearly all. Satan works craftily to take God's Word and weave in false doctrine here and there to accomplish his agenda.

> Galatians 5:9 - A little leaven leaveneth the whole lump.

> 1 Corinthians 5:6b - Know ye not that a little leaven leaveneth the whole lump?

Although modern versions have some truth, that does not mean one should use them when there are clear errors.

> Matthew 4:4 - But he answered and said, It is written, Man shall not live by bread alone, but by every word that proceedeth out of the mouth of God.

> Luke 4:4 - And Jesus answered him, saying, It is written, That man shall not live by bread alone, but by every word of God.

We cannot live by every Word of God if modern versions change thousands of God's Words. We must trust in the fact that the Word of God is available today as promised and that it is alive and powerful.

> Hebrews 4:12 - For the word of God *is* quick, and powerful, and sharper than any twoedged sword, piercing even to the dividing asunder of soul and spirit, and of the joints and marrow, and *is* a discerner of the thoughts and intents of the heart.

6. Are Modern Versions Easier to Understand?

It is commonly thought that modern versions are easier to understand and that the King James Bible uses too many archaic and complicated words. While modern versions may be easier to read in some instances, they are not as clear as the KJV and often confusing.

Some read the KJV and are bothered that they do not understand certain words, so they turn to man's paraphrases instead of seeking to understand God's Holy Word. Even though there might be a few words that we do not immediately understand, that does not mean we should switch to a different version. Let us look at an example God provided of how to handle so-called outdated words.

> 1 Samuel 9:9 - (Beforetime in Israel, when a man went to enquire of God, thus he spake, Come, and let us go to the seer: for *he that is* now *called* a Prophet was beforetime called a Seer.)

In 1 Samuel 9, Saul and one of his father's servants go to the seer to seek help. God dedicates an entire verse to explain how we should view archaic words. Verse 9 explains that the unfamiliar word "seer" means the same thing as the more familiar word "prophet." God did not delete the archaic word. He left it in and explained the meaning. The solution to archaic words is not to get a modern version that removes them but to study context and cross references to grasp the meaning.

It is sometimes said that modern versions simplify the complexity of the KJV. This is not entirely true. In many cases, modern versions will incorporate words that are more common today but leave out key details necessary for understanding. While some may not be used to the English of the KJV, it should not be discarded simply because of lack of familiarity.

Admittedly, understanding the Bible can and will be difficult at times, but God is not the author of confusion. He authored a living book that perceives and discerns our intents. We are commanded to study and rightly divide God's Word to show ourselves approved.

> 1 Corinthians 14:33 - For God is not *the author* of confusion, but of peace, as in all churches of the saints.
>
> Hebrews 4:12 - For the word of God *is* quick, and powerful, and sharper than any twoedged sword, piercing even to the dividing asunder of soul and spirit, and of the joints and marrow, and *is* a discerner of the thoughts and intents of the heart.
>
> 2 Timothy 2:15 - Study to shew thyself approved unto God, a workman that needeth not to be ashamed, rightly dividing the word of truth.

The Bible is understandable but not always direct. If one seeks to understand God's Word and studies it, one will ultimately find the truth.

7. Why Are There So Many Modern Versions?

Paul warns of deception and false letters written in his name back in the first century. He refers to those who produce them as those which corrupt the Word of God. That many do not realize the vast scope of the deception is a sign of how well it is working. It is logical to conclude that over the past two thousand years Satan's deceptions have multiplied. The simple fact that many do not understand where God's Word is today shows the magnitude of Satan's influence.

> 2 Thessalonians 2:2 - That ye be not soon shaken in mind, or be troubled, neither by spirit, nor by word, nor by letter as from us, as that the day of Christ is at hand.

> 2 Corinthians 2:17 - For we are not as many, which corrupt the word of God: but as of sincerity, but as of God, in the sight of God speak we in Christ.

> 2 Timothy 3:13 - But evil men and seducers shall wax worse and worse, deceiving, and being deceived.

Modern versions are the evident handiwork of Satan to subvert and corrupt God's Word and to circulate his false doctrine as a substitute. Information today is often presented as truth, when in actuality, it is falsehood and deceit (Col. 2:8). 1 Timothy 6:20 similarly warns of "science falsely so called."

Modern versions change and corrupt God's Word, perhaps motivated by money and/or renown.

> 1 Timothy 6:10 - For the love of money is the root of

all evil: which while some coveted after, they have erred from the faith, and pierced themselves through with many sorrows.

Matthew 23:5-7 - But all their works they do for to be seen of men: they make broad their phylacteries, and enlarge the borders of their garments, 6) And love the uppermost rooms at feasts, and the chief seats in the synagogues, 7) And greetings in the markets, and to be called of men, Rabbi, Rabbi.

It is imperative that translators heed the following warnings before setting out to translate the Word of God.

Deuteronomy 4:2 - Ye shall not add unto the word which I command you, neither shall ye diminish *ought* from it, that ye may keep the commandments of the LORD your God which I command you.

Deuteronomy 12:32 - What thing soever I command you, observe to do it: thou shalt not add thereto, nor diminish from it.

Proverbs 30:5-6 - Every word of God *is* pure: he *is* a shield unto them that put their trust in him. 6) Add thou not unto his words, lest he reprove thee, and thou be found a liar.

Revelation 22:18-19 - For I testify unto every man that heareth the words of the prophecy of this book, If any man shall add unto these things, God shall add unto him the plagues that are written in this book: 19) And if any man shall take away from the words of the book of this prophecy, God shall take away his part out of the book of life, and out of the holy city, and *from* the things which are written in this book.

It is no coincidence that there are so many newer versions of the Bible that are alleged to be more accurate and easier to understand. It is obvious from observing their errors that they are counterfeits of the promised and preserved Word of God today: the King James Bible.

8. Should One Trust the King James Bible over the Hebrew and Greek Interpretations of Scholars?

The KJV has been proven to be more accurate than all modern versions of the Bible, but should one have confidence in it over the Hebrew and Greek interpretations of scholars?

1. God's promise of preservation and His faithfulness to all generations.

God promised many times to preserve His Word.

> Psalm 12:6-7 - The words of the LORD *are* pure words: *as* silver tried in a furnace of earth, purified seven times. 7) Thou shalt keep them, O LORD, thou shalt preserve them from this generation for ever.

> Isaiah 40:8 - The grass withereth, the flower fadeth: but the word of our God shall stand for ever.

> Matthew 5:18 - For verily I say unto you, Till heaven and earth pass, one jot or one tittle shall in no wise pass from the law, till all be fulfilled.

> Matthew 24:35 - Heaven and earth shall pass away, but my words shall not pass away.

> Mark 13:31 - Heaven and earth shall pass away: but my words shall not pass away.

Luke 16:17 - And it is easier for heaven and earth to pass, than one tittle of the law to fail.

Luke 21:33 - Heaven and earth shall pass away: but my words shall not pass away.

1 Peter 1:25 - But the word of the Lord endureth for ever. And this is the word which by the gospel is preached unto you.

If it is necessary to know both Biblical Hebrew and Greek to understand the Scriptures, then God has restricted His Word to an elite academic few that consists of less than .01% of the earth's population. Does God restrict His Word to the scholars, or does he intend it for the common man? In pondering this question, consider the Lord's view of the elite academics of His day – the scribes and Pharisees.

Matthew 15:12-14 - Then came his disciples, and said unto him, Knowest thou that the **Pharisees** were offended, after they heard this saying? 13) But he answered and said, Every plant, which my heavenly Father hath not planted, shall be rooted up. 14) Let them alone: they be **blind leaders of the blind. And if the blind lead the blind, both shall fall into the ditch.**

Matthew 23:15-17 - Woe unto you, **scribes and Pharisees**, hypocrites! for ye compass sea and land to make one proselyte, and when he is made, ye make him twofold more the child of hell than yourselves. 16) Woe unto you, *ye* **blind guides**, which say, Whosoever shall swear by the temple, it is nothing; but whosoever shall swear by the gold of the temple, he is a debtor! 17) Ye **fools and blind**: for whether is greater, the gold, or the temple that sanctifieth the gold?

Matthew 23:19 - Ye **fools and blind**: for whether *is* greater, the gift, or the altar that sanctifieth the gift?

> Matthew 23:23 - Woe unto you, **scribes and Pharisees**, hypocrites! for ye pay tithe of mint and anise and cummin, and have omitted the weightier *matters* of the law, judgment, mercy, and faith: these ought ye to have done, and not to leave the other undone. 24) Ye **blind guides**, which strain at a gnat, and swallow a camel.

It is logical to conclude that God perpetuated His Word by having it translated into English, the most spoken language on Earth. If all modern versions of the Bible have clear errors, which they do, and the KJV does not, then this proves the KJV is the promised, preserved Word of God for English-speaking people today.

If God is faithful to all generations, then His perfect Word must be available to all generations.

> Psalm 33:11 - The counsel of the LORD standeth for ever, the thoughts of his heart to all generations.

> Psalm 100:5 - For the LORD *is* good; his mercy *is* everlasting; and his truth *endureth* to all generations.

> Psalm 119:89-90 - LAMED. For ever, O LORD, thy word is settled in heaven. 90) Thy faithfulness *is* unto all generations: thou hast established the earth, and it abideth.

> Psalm 119:160 - Thy word *is* true *from* the beginning: and every one of thy righteous judgments *endureth* for ever.

> Isaiah 59:21 - As for me, this *is* my covenant with them, saith the LORD; My spirit that *is* upon thee, and my words which I have put in thy mouth, shall not depart out of thy mouth, nor out of the mouth of thy seed, nor out of the mouth of thy seed's seed, saith the LORD, from henceforth and for ever.

2. God has worked through His Word in common language throughout time to give understanding.

Exodus 17:14 - And the LORD said unto Moses, Write this *for* a memorial in a book, and rehearse *it* in the ears of Joshua: for I will utterly put out the remembrance of Amalek from under heaven.

Deuteronomy 11:18-20 - Therefore shall ye lay up these my words in your heart and in your soul, and bind them for a sign upon your hand, that they may be as frontlets between your eyes. 19) And ye shall teach them your children, speaking of them when thou sittest in thine house, and when thou walkest by the way, when thou liest down, and when thou risest up. 20) And thou shalt write them upon the door posts of thine house, and upon thy gates:

The written word is so important that the king of Israel was commanded to write himself a personal copy of the law and read it so "that he may learn to fear the LORD his God."

Deuteronomy 17:18-19 - And it shall be, when he sitteth upon the throne of his kingdom, that he shall write him a copy of this law in a book out of *that which is* before the priests the Levites: 19) And it shall be with him, and he shall read therein all the days of his life: that he may learn to fear the LORD his God, to keep all the words of this law and these statutes, to do them:

The examples below show that God places a high emphasis on the penned form of His word. Without such copies of His word, there would be doubt as to what God really said and the Word of God would lose its authority.

Isaiah 30:8 - Now go, write it before them in a table, and note it in a book, that it may be for the time to come for ever and ever:

Psalm 68:11 - The Lord gave the word: great *was* the company of those that published *it*.

Jeremiah 30:2 - Thus speaketh the LORD God of Israel, saying, Write thee all the words that I have spoken unto thee in a book.

Daniel 10:21 - But I will shew thee that which is noted in the scripture of truth: and *there is* none that holdeth with me in these things, but Michael your prince.

Habakkuk 2:2 - And the LORD answered me, and said, Write the vision, and make *it* plain upon tables, that he may run that readeth it.

Romans 15:4 - For whatsoever things were written aforetime were written for our learning, that we through patience and comfort of the scriptures might have hope.

Revelation 1:1-3 - The Revelation of Jesus Christ, which God gave unto him, to shew unto his servants things which must shortly come to pass; and he sent and signified *it* by his angel unto his servant John: 2) Who bare record of the word of God, and of the testimony of Jesus Christ, and of all things that he saw. 3) Blessed *is* he that readeth, and they that hear the words of this prophecy, and keep those things which are written therein: for the time *is* at hand.

Revelation 21:5 - And he that sat upon the throne said, Behold, I make all things new. And he said unto me, Write: for these words are true and faithful.

It is worth noting that having a multitude of copies of the Word of God prevents it from being destroyed completely as Jehudi tried to do in Jeremiah 36.

Jeremiah 36:23 - And it came to pass, *that* when Jehudi had read three or four leaves, he cut it with the penknife, and cast *it* into the fire that *was* on the hearth, until all the roll was consumed in the fire that *was* on the hearth.

Jehudi's attempt failed as God simply recreated the roll that was destroyed and added new words, documenting Jehudi's wrongdoings.

> Jeremiah 36:32 - Then took Jeremiah another roll, and gave it to Baruch the scribe, the son of Neriah; who wrote therein from the mouth of Jeremiah all the words of the book which Jehoiakim king of Judah had burned in the fire: and there were added besides unto them many like words.

3. We are commanded to meditate upon the Word of God, hide it in our hearts, keep it, study it, hold fast to it, desire it, and let it dwell in us richly. All of these commands are meaningless, nonsensical, and impossible to perform if we do not have an accessible Bible.

> Joshua 1:8 - This book of the law shall not depart out of thy mouth; but thou shalt meditate therein day and night, that thou mayest observe to do according to all that is written therein: for then thou shalt make thy way prosperous, and then thou shalt have good success.

> Psalm 119:11 - Thy word have I hid in mine heart, that I might not sin against thee.

> Psalm 119:15-16 - I will meditate in thy precepts, and have respect unto thy ways. 16) I will delight myself in thy statutes: I will not forget thy word.

> Psalm 119:48 - My hands also will I lift up unto thy commandments, which I have loved; and I will meditate in thy statutes.

> Psalm 119:78 - Let the proud be ashamed; for they dealt perversely with me without a cause: *but* I will meditate in thy precepts.

Psalm 119:105 - NUN. Thy word *is* a lamp unto my feet, and a light unto my path.

Psalm 119:130 - The entrance of thy words giveth light; it giveth understanding unto the simple.

Psalm 119:148 - Mine eyes prevent the *night* watches, that I might meditate in thy word.

Jeremiah 15:16 - Thy words were found, and I did eat them; and thy word was unto me the joy and rejoicing of mine heart: for I am called by thy name, O LORD God of hosts.

Luke 8:15 - But that on the good ground are they, which in an honest and good heart, having heard the word, keep *it*, and bring forth fruit with patience.

Colossians 3:16 - Let the word of Christ dwell in you richly in all wisdom; teaching and admonishing one another in psalms and hymns and spiritual songs, singing with grace in your hearts to the Lord.

1 Timothy 4:15 - Meditate upon these things; give thyself wholly to them; that thy profiting may appear to all.

2 Timothy 2:15 - Study to shew thyself approved unto God, a workman that needeth not to be ashamed, rightly dividing the word of truth.

Titus 1:9 - Holding fast the faithful word as he hath been taught, that he may be able by sound doctrine both to exhort and to convince the gainsayers.

1 Peter 2:2 - As newborn babes, desire the sincere milk of the word, that ye may grow thereby:

How is it possible to meditate on and let the Word of Christ dwell in us richly if most cannot even read or understand it? The Word of God is our light and our guide, and we must be able to know what it says if we are to allow it to work in and through us.

4. God makes the truth understandable and available to all so that they are without excuse and can be held accountable.

Deuteronomy 30:11-14 - For this commandment which I command thee this day, it is not hidden from thee, neither is it far off. 12) It is not in heaven, that thou shouldest say, Who shall go up for us to heaven, and bring it unto us, that we may hear it, and do it? 13) Neither is it beyond the sea, that thou shouldest say, Who shall go over the sea for us, and bring it unto us, that we may hear it, and do it? 14) But the word is very nigh unto thee, in thy mouth, and in thy heart, that thou mayest do it.

Psalm 19:1-4 - [[To the chief Musician, A Psalm of David.]] The heavens declare the glory of God; and the firmament sheweth his handywork. 2) Day unto day uttereth speech, and night unto night sheweth knowledge. 3) There is no speech nor language, where their voice is not heard. 4) Their line is gone out through all the earth, and their words to the end of the world. In them hath he set a tabernacle for the sun,

Romans 1:20 - For the invisible things of him from the creation of the world are clearly seen, being understood by the things that are made, even his eternal power and Godhead; so that they are without excuse:

Romans 10:8 - But what saith it? The word is nigh thee, even in thy mouth, and in thy heart: that is, the word of faith, which we preach;

According to Romans 1:20, all are without excuse. The guilty will not be able to say that God did not give them enough evidence to believe. God did not leave His Word in the largely inaccessible Hebrew and Greek languages. Rather, He translated it so it is available in the common language of man today. The Word of God is not difficult to find or unobtainable. People have access to it according to Romans 1:18, but they hold it in unrighteousness and disregard it.

Romans 1:18 - For the wrath of God is revealed from heaven against all ungodliness and unrighteousness of men, who hold the truth in unrighteousness;

5. God's repeated warnings not to add to or subtract from His Word necessitate that His Word must exist and be available to be corrupted or else such commands are irrelevant.

Deuteronomy 4:2 - Ye shall not add unto the word which I command you, neither shall ye diminish *ought* from it, that ye may keep the commandments of the LORD your God which I command you.

Deuteronomy 12:32 - What thing soever I command you, observe to do it: thou shalt not add thereto, nor diminish from it.

Proverbs 30:5-6 - Every word of God *is* pure: he *is* a shield unto them that put their trust in him. 6) Add thou not unto his words, lest he reprove thee, and thou be found a liar.

Revelation 22:19 - And if any man shall take away from the words of the book of this prophecy, God shall take away his part out of the book of life, and out of the holy city, and *from* the things which are written in this book.

For these reasons, one can have confidence in the King James Bible over the Hebrew and Greek interpretations of scholars. For it is better to trust in the LORD than to put confidence in man (Ps. 118:8).

9. Why so Few Believe in the King James Version

1. Humanity has free will and God allows for unbelief.

The Bible is written with just enough ambiguity to allow all to believe as they choose. If it were possible to prove the infallibility of the King James Bible as an undeniable fact, we would not walk by faith but by sight.

> Hebrews 11:6 - But without faith *it is* impossible to please *him*: for he that cometh to God must believe that he is, and *that* he is a rewarder of them that diligently seek him.

> Hebrews 4:12 - For the word of God *is* quick, and powerful, and sharper than any twoedged sword, piercing even to the dividing asunder of soul and spirit, and of the joints and marrow, and *is* a discerner of the thoughts and intents of the heart.

> Proverbs 5:21 - For the ways of man *are* before the eyes of the LORD, and he pondereth all his goings.

> Proverbs 21:2 - Every way of a man *is* right in his own eyes: but the LORD pondereth the hearts.

The Word of God is alive and knows our intents. When one seeks wisdom in the Word of God, one will find it. When a doubter seeks to find fault in the Bible, he will be able to find seeming reasons to disbelieve as God will answer him according to the idols of his heart. (Ez. 14:3-5)

2. Deception

There is an immense amount of confusion due to the deception of the world. Most people are not rooted in the truth and are thus easily deceived.

> 2 Corinthians 4:4 - In whom the god of this world hath blinded the minds of them which believe not, lest the light of the glorious gospel of Christ, who is the image of God, should shine unto them.

> Ephesians 4:14 - That we *henceforth* be no more children, tossed to and fro, and carried about with every wind of doctrine, by the sleight of men, *and* cunning craftiness, whereby they lie in wait to deceive;

> 2 Timothy 3:13 - But evil men and seducers shall wax worse and worse, deceiving, and being deceived.

3. The truth will always be despised.

> Proverbs 1:22 - How long, ye simple ones, will ye love simplicity? and the scorners delight in their scorning, and fools hate knowledge?

> Proverbs 18:2 - A fool hath no delight in understanding, but that his heart may discover itself.

> Proverbs 23:9 - Speak not in the ears of a fool: for he will despise the wisdom of thy words.

> 1 Corinthians 1:18 - For the preaching of the cross is to them that perish foolishness; but unto us which are saved it is the power of God.

> Galatians 4:16 - Am I therefore become your enemy, because I tell you the truth?

4. The majority will consistently be wrong and never come unto the knowledge of the truth (1 Tim. 2:4).

Matthew 7:13-14 - Enter ye in at the strait gate: for wide *is* the gate, and broad *is* the way, that leadeth to destruction, and many there be which go in thereat: 14) Because strait *is* the gate, and narrow *is* the way, which leadeth unto life, and few there be that find it.

Matthew 22:14 - For many are called, but few *are* chosen.

The majority of people during the Lord's time on earth did not believe. Only eight got onto the ark after a hundred and twenty years of warning. The majority of Israel worshipped Aaron's calf in Exodus 32, and nearly all of Israel rejected the prophets. The majority will always be incorrect. However, the majority does not determine truth. We thank God that He has not left us without witness but has preserved His Word in the KJV.

10. Conclusion

The purpose of this book is to demonstrate the definitive authority of the King James Version as God's Word today. Presented with Biblical proof, the following points were established:

1. It is essential to the believer's faith to be able to determine where God's Word is today.

2. Satan aims to undermine God's Word.

3. Modern versions contain many differences and errors while the KJV is without error, precise, and trustworthy.

4. Recognizing the errors in modern versions and not simply viewing them as inconsequential variations is key to pinpointing which Bible is truly accurate.

5. While modern versions profess to be easier to understand, they are not.

6. Modern versions are counterfeits of God's Word.

7. One can have faith in the King James Bible and not worry about the Hebrew and Greek interpretations of scholars.

8. The popular solution is not always right. Even though many will disregard the KJV, one can be confident that it is God's Word.

With this understanding, you are hopefully one step closer to coming unto the knowledge of the truth (1 Tim. 2:4). Study these issues and decide what you personally believe. Satisfy yourself with the truth and do not simply take someone's word for it.

2 Timothy 2:15 - Study to shew thyself approved unto God, a workman that needeth not to be ashamed, rightly dividing the word of truth.

Finally, we all should strive to be like those in Berea as they searched the Scriptures daily.

Acts 17:10-11 - And the brethren immediately sent away Paul and Silas by night unto Berea: who coming *thither* went into the synagogue of the Jews. 11) These were more noble than those in Thessalonica, in that they received the word with all readiness of mind, and searched the scriptures daily, whether those things were so.

We pray that you find this study edifying and that the God of our Lord Jesus Christ give unto you the spirit of wisdom and revelation in the knowledge of him (Eph. 1:17).

2 Corinthians 1:24 - Not for that we have dominion over your faith, but are helpers of your joy: for by faith ye stand.

Dispensational Publishing House is striving to become the go-to source for Bible-based materials from the dispensational perspective.

Our goal is to provide high-quality doctrinal and worldview resources that make dispensational theology accessible to people at all levels of understanding.

Visit our blog regularly to read informative articles from both known and new writers.

And please let us know how we can better serve you.

Dispensational Publishing House, Inc.
PO Box 3181
Taos, NM 87571

Call us toll free 844-321-4202

www.DispensationalPublishing.com